Traverse Theatre Company

GIRL
IN
THE
MACHINE

BY STEF SMITH

First performed at the Traverse Theatre, Edinburgh,
on 5 April 2017

A Traverse Theatre Company Commission

Company

OWEN	Michael Dylan
POLLY	Rosalind Sydney
VOICE	Victoria Liddelle
Director	Orla O'Loughlin
Designer	Neil Warmington
Lighting Designer	Sergey Jakovsky
Composer/Sound Designer	Kim Moore
Choreography	White & Givan
Assistant Director	Nikki Kalkman
Production Manager	Kevin McCallum
Chief Electrician	Renny Robertson
Deputy Electrician	Claire Elliot
Head of Stage	Gary Staerck
Lighting & Sound Technician	Tom Saunders
Stage Manager	Danni Bastian
Deputy Stage Manager	Gillian Richards
Assistant Stage Manager	Shellie Barrowcliffe
Costume Supervisor	Sophie Ferguson

Biographies

Michael Dylan (OWEN)
Michael Dylan trained at the Guildhall School of Music and Drama.

His work in theatre includes: *The Lonesome West* (Tron Theatre/Russian tour); *One Man, Two Guvnors* (National Theatre/UK and Ireland tour); *Ulysses* (Tron Theatre/Edinburgh Festival Fringe/Irish tour); *Mikey and Addie* (macrobert/Imaginate); *A Midsummer Night's Dream* (Headlong); *Comedians* (Lyric Hammersmith); *Moonshadow* (White Bear Theatre); *Black Comedy* (Bridewell Theatre); *Deirdre of the Sorrows* (Irish national tour).

Film/TV credits include: *Shetland* (BBC Scotland); *Big Brother: Secrets and Lies* (Endemol); *Bert and Dickie* (BBC); *Muppets Most Wanted* (Disney); *For George*; *Ash Wednesday*.

Michael recently won the Best Male Actor Award at the International Martin McDonagh Festival in Russia for his role as Father Welsh in *The Lonesome West* (Tron Theatre).

Sergey Jakovsky (Lighting Designer)
Originally from St Petersburg, Sergey was born into a family of two theatre directors and has an extensive background in theatre and arts.

He trained at the Royal Scottish Academy of Music and Drama, Glasgow, and graduated with a BA in Technical and Production Arts.

Sergey has worked for a variety of creative industries within the UK and Europe, including theatre, contemporary dance and installation arts, designing for companies such as Dundee Rep, Tron Theatre, Catherine Wheels, Grid Iron, Derevo Theatre Company, Traverse Theatre, Communicado and Sharmanka Kinetic Theatre.

Victoria Liddelle (VOICE)
Previous work at the Traverse includes: *Pandas, The Last Witch, Kyoto* and *The King of the Fields*. Other theatre includes: *Sandiago* (Tron Theatre); *Casanova* (Suspect Culture); *Passing Places* (Derby Playhouse); *Britannia Rules* and *The Snow Queen* (Royal Lyceum Theatre Edinburgh).

TV credits include: *The Loch* (ITV); *Eve* (CBBC); *Scot Squad, River City, The Crash, Bob Servant, Case Histories* (BBC). Radio includes: *The Pillow Book, The Whole of the Moon, The Gowk Storm, The Golden Slipper, Himmler's Boy, Dr Korzack* (BBC).

Kim Moore (Composer/Sound Designer)
Kim Moore studied Music at Glasgow University before joining indie pop band Zoey Van Goey. Since then Kim has collaborated across experimental electronic and contemporary music in projects for dance, theatre and film. She also produces music under the name WOLF.

Recent/current work includes: Fringe First winner *Faslane* (Jenna Watt); *Blow Off* (AJ Taudevin); *Little Red* (Barrowland Ballet); *Birdbones* (Peter Lannon and Ellie Dubois); *My Music* (Magnetic North); *Scream, Moth Death EP* (WOLF); *Blow Off* album recording and production. International work includes: *Tigertale/Tiger* (Barrowland Ballet/international touring in China, Australia, Japan, Egypt and Europe). Previous work includes: *Hell Unltd* (Glasgow Film Theatre); *Dolls* (National Theatre of Scotland); *Sex and God* (Magnetic North); *Edgelands*

(Adopt a Composer and Bristol Reggae Orchestra); *Cycling Gymkhana* (Eilidh MacAskill); *Purposeless Movements* (Birds of Paradise); *Icepole, Blueblock Studio, Sprogrock* (Katy Wilson and Starcatchers); *Un Petit Molière* (Lung Ha Theatre Company).

Film includes: *V-day* (Lucas Kao); *Hell Unltd* (Glasgow Film Theatre).

Exhibitions/installations include: *We Run We Walk We Run* (Glasgow Women's Library); *To Sail Among the Billows* (Glasgow City Hall); *The Forgotten Island* (GIANT); *This Is Where I Got To* (Buzzcut).

Recording/producing: *The Cage Was Unlocked All Along, Propeller versus Wings* (Zoey Van Goey); *Church Bells Tide Out* (Concrete Antenna); *Jogalong Remix* (Rozi Plain); *Luxury Discovery Remix* (Miaoux Miaoux); *The Last Fall, Black Rabbit* (WOLF). Performing/collaborating on records and live performances with Lord Cutglass, Frightened Rabbit, Sound of Yell, PHOENE, John Lemke, Dave Clark and Tony Bevan.

Orla O'Loughlin (Director)
Orla is Artistic Director of the Traverse Theatre. Prior to this she was Artistic Director of Pentabus Theatre and International Associate at the Royal Court. Over the course of her career she has directed an eclectic mix of award-winning and internationally acclaimed new work at a range of arts venues, festivals and non-conventional theatre spaces.

Directing work for the Traverse includes: *Grain in The Blood, Milk, A Respectable Widow Takes to Vulgarity, Clean, The Artist Man and The Mother Woman,* The Scotsman Fringe First and Scottish Arts Club award-winning *Swallow,* the Scotsman Fringe First, Herald Angel and CATS award-winning *Ciara,* the Scotsman Fringe First award-winning *Spoiling,* and the Herald Angel award-winning *Dream Plays (Scenes from a Play I'll Never Write).* Other theatre includes: *How Much is your Iron?* (Young Vic); *The Hound of the Baskervilles* (West Yorkshire Playhouse/West End); *Kebab* (Dublin International Theatre Festival/Royal Court Theatre); *For Once* (Hampstead Theatre); *Underland* (performed 200 feet below ground in Clearwell Caves); *Shuffle* (performed by a cast of 70 in Merry Hill – Europe's largest shopping centre).

Orla is a former recipient of the James Menzies Kitchin Award and the Carlton Bursary at the Donmar Warehouse. She was listed in the *Observer* as one of the top 50 Cultural leaders in the UK.

Stef Smith (Writer)
Stef Smith is an Associate Artist of the Traverse Theatre. Her work includes *Swallow* (Traverse Theatre); *Human Animals* (Royal Court Theatre); *Remote* (NT Connections); *And the Beat Goes On* (Random Accomplice/Horsecross); *Grey Matter* (Lemon Tree); *Falling/Flying* (Tron Theatre) and *Roadkill* (Pachamama Productions). She was awarded an Olivier Award for Outstanding Achievement in an Affiliate Theatre, Best New Production, Critics' Award for Theatre in Scotland, Amnesty International Expression of Freedom Award, Herald Angel, Total Theatre Award and Fringe First Award for *Roadkill*; and the Scottish Arts Club Theatre Award and Fringe First Award for *Swallow.*

Rosalind Sydney (POLLY)
Rosalind Sydney trained at Royal Conservatoire of Scotland.

Recent theatre credits include: *The Night After Christmas* (Tron Theatre); *Invisible Army* (Terra Incognita); *Billy* (*The Days of Howling*), *Faster Louder, The Misanthrope* (Òran Mór); *News Just In* (Random Accomplice); *Appointment with the Wickerman, The Day I Swapped My Dad for Two Goldfish* (National Theatre of Scotland); *Rough Cuts* (Royal Court Theatre); *My Romantic History* (Bush Theatre); *Interiors, Subway, The Beggar's Opera* (Vanishing Point); *Sleeping Beauty* (Citizens Theatre); *Pobby and Dingan, Caged, Snow Baby, Cyrano* (Catherine Wheels Theatre Company).

Film/TV credits include: *Bob Servant* (BBC4) and *Things That Are Important to Us* (Little Viking). Rosalind performs regularly in radio drama with BBC Radio, and recently read extracts for BBC Radio 4's *With Great Pleasure*.

Her play *Up To Speed* will go out on tour later this year under the Imaginate/National Theatre of Scotland's *Theatre in Schools* initiative.

Neil Warmington (Designer)
Neil graduated in Fine Art from Maidstone College of Art before attending the Motley Theatre Design Course in London.

Work for the Traverse includes: *I'm With the Band, The Dark Things, Full Moon for a Solemn Mass* (with the Barbican), *Passing Places, King of the Fields, Gagarin Way,* and *The Slab Boys Trilogy.*

Other theatre credits include: *Fever Dream: Southside* (Citizens Theatre); *Ghosts* (Tron Theatre); *The Missing, Mary Stuart, Elizabeth Gordon Quinn* (National Theatre of Scotland); *Death of a Salesman, Further Than The Furthest Thing, Romeo and Juliet, Sunshine on Leith, If Destroyed True, Gypsy, Scenes from an Execution, Dumbstruck, A Christmas Carol, Cinderella, Jack and the Beanstalk, Victoria, The Talented Mr Ripley, Lie of the Mind* (Dundee Rep); *The Straits, The Drowned World, Helmet, Splendour, Riddance, The Small Things, This Other England, Pyrenees* (Paines Plough); *King Lear, Ghosts, Don Juan, The Taming of the Shrew, Love's Labour's Lost* (English Touring Theatre); *The Vortex* (Rose Theatre); *Woyzeck, The Glass Menagerie, Comedians, Arsenic and Old Lace* (Royal Lyceum Theatre Edinburgh); *Life's a Dream, Fiddler on the Roof, Playhouse Creatures* (West Yorkshire Playhouse); *Henry V* (Royal Shakespeare Company); *Much Ado About Nothing* (Queen's Theatre, London); *The Life of Stuff* (Donmar Warehouse); *Jane Eyre, Desire Under the Elms* (Shared Experience); *Sunset Song, Mary Queen of Scots Got Her Head Chopped Off* (Prime Productions); *Much Ado About Nothing, Waiting for Godot* (Liverpool Everyman); *The Tempest* (Contact) Theatre; *Troilus & Cressida* (Opera North); *Oedipus Rex ,The Marriage of Figaro* (Garsington Opera); *The Caretaker, Knives in Hens* (TAG); *Angels in America* (7:84); *Top Girls* (RADA Teaching).

Neil has also received four TMA Awards, a CATS Award for Best Design and The Linbury Prize for stage design, and designed the 1999 Year of Culture launch at the Armadillo.

White & Givan (Choreography)
Previous choreography work for the Traverse includes: *Grain in the Blood, Milk, Tracks of the Winter Bear* and *Swallow*. As performers and choreographers with over twenty-five years of experience, White & Givan Co-Artistic Directors Errol White and Davina Givan have a wealth of experience they have fed into the company since its inception in 2009 under its former name, Errol White Company. They have both performed internationally for many years, working alongside such distinguished directors and choreographers as Rui Horta, Darshan Singh Buller, Richard Alston, Wayne McGregor, Bob Cohan, and Janet Smith among many others. In addition to their extensive performing and repertory work they are respected and valued education practitioners, having spent five years as Artistic and Creative Directors of National Youth Dance Wales, and have taught extensively across the UK. Since 2009 the company has received generous support from Creative Scotland, which has allowed Errol and Davina to share their artistic work and practitioner experience with the Scottish dance community. They've staged three successful and critically acclaimed Scottish tours of *Three Works, IAM* and most recently *Breathe.* They are currently engaged in a unique dance-company-in-residence scheme with the University of Edinburgh.

Nikki Kalkman (Assistant Director) *Leverhulme Arts Scholar and Recipient of the JMK Regional Assistant Director Bursary*

Nikki is an independent theatremaker, director and producer with a background in physical theatre, puppetry and visual theatre. Since graduating with a Bachelor in Creative Industries (Drama) in Brisbane, she has worked extensively in both Australian and UK theatre.

A co-founder of physical theatre ensemble Choral Jam she directed and produced their first theatre piece *The Body In Shadow* at manipulate 2017 with support from Creative Scotland. Other directing work includes: solo object manipulation performance *Mrs. Jordan* (Festival Mondial Des Théâtres De Marionnettes/Hidden Door) and Lesley Wilson's *A Woman, A Crow, A Giant and A Field* (Tron 100 Festival 2016). She has also worked as the Assistant Director for Strange Town Youth Theatre's *What Now?* presented at the Traverse in June 2016. In October 2016 Nikki travelled to Montreal, Canada to work on Marcelle Hudon's *L'Effet Hyde* (Théâtre aux Écuries).

Nikki often works with young people running specialty workshops in drama and puppetry, she is an active member of the the Tron 100 Club, Traverse Directors Programme and has participated in the FST mentorship programme.

Traverse Theatre Company

The Traverse is Scotland's new writing theatre.

Formed in 1963 by a group of passionate theatre enthusiasts, the Traverse was founded to extend the spirit of the Edinburgh festivals throughout the year. Today, under Artistic Director Orla O'Loughlin, the Traverse nurtures emerging talent, produces award-winning new plays and offers a curated programme of the best work from the UK and beyond, spanning theatre, dance, performance, music and spoken word.

The Traverse has launched the careers of some of the UK's most celebrated writers – David Greig, David Harrower and Zinnie Harris – and continues to discover and support new voices – Stef Smith, Morna Pearson, Gary McNair and Rob Drummond.

With two custom-built and versatile theatre spaces, the Traverse's home in Edinburgh's city centre is a powerhouse of vibrant new work for, and of, our time. Every August, it holds an iconic status as the theatrical heart of the Edinburgh Festival Fringe.

Outside the theatre walls, it runs an extensive engagement programme, offering audiences of all ages and backgrounds the opportunity to explore, create and develop. Further afield, the Traverse frequently tours internationally and engages in exchanges and partnerships – most recently in Quebec, New Zealand and South Korea.

'The Traverse remains the best new writing theatre in Britain.' *Guardian*

For more information about the Traverse please visit **traverse.co.uk**.

With thanks

The Traverse Theatre extends grateful thanks to all those who generously support our work, including those who prefer their support to remain anonymous.

Traverse Theatre Supporters
Diamond – Alan & Penny Barr, Katie Bradford
Platinum – Angus McLeod, Iain Millar, Nicholas & Lesley Pryor, David Rodgers
Gold – Carola Bronte-Stewart, Helen Pitkethly
Silver – Judy & Steve, Bridget M Stevens, Allan Wilson
Bronze – Barbara Cartwright

Trusts and Foundations
The Andrew Lloyd Webber Foundation
The Backstage Trust
The Cross Trust
The Dr David Summers Charitable Trust
The James Menzies-Kitchin Memorial Trust
The Linbury Trust
Santander Foundation
The Unity Theatre Trust
The W. M. Mann Foundation
The Saltire Society Trust

Corporate Supporter
Arthur McKay

Traverse Theatre Production Supporters
Cotterell & Co
Paterson SA Hairdressing
Black Box Signs
Allander Print

Special thanks go to Zinnie Harris, Amy Gilmartin, Martin McCormick, Kirsty Stuart, Jon Oberlander and the University of Edinburgh, St. Columba's Hospice, Mandy Laurie and Edinburgh International Science Festival

ALBA | CHRUTHACHAIL

Traverse Theatre (Scotland) is a Limited Company (SC076037) and a Scottish Charity (SC002368) with its Registered Office at 10 Cambridge Street, Edinburgh, Scotland, EH1 2ED.

Traverse Theatre

The Company

Linda Crooks	Executive Producer & Joint Chief Executive
Isobel Dew	Administrator
David Drummond	General Manager
Claire Elliot	Deputy Electrician
Sarah Farrell	Box Office Supervisor
Ellen Gledhill	Development Manager
Tom Grayson	Box Office Manager
Zinnie Harris	Associate Director
Rosie Kellagher	Literary Associate
Rebecca Kirby	Deputy Box Office Manager
Rebecca Low	Box Office Supervisor
Kath Lowe	Front of House Manager
Catherine Makin	Artistic Administrator
Kevin McCallum	Head of Production
Bradley McCathie	Bar Café Senior Supervisor
Ruth McEwan	Producer
Lauren McLay	Marketing & Communications Assistant
Victoria Murray	Head of Communications
Ondine Oberlin	Box Office Supervisor
Orla O'Loughlin	Artistic Director & Joint Chief Executive
Julie Pigott	Head of Finance & Operations
Pauleen Rafferty	Payroll & HR Manager
Sunniva Ramsay	Engagement Manager
Renny Robertson	Chief Electrician
Michelle Sandham	Finance Officer
Tom Saunders	Lighting & Sound Technician
Dean Scott	Head Chef
Gary Staerck	Head of Stage
Kyriakos Vogiatzis	Marketing & Campaigns Officer
Emily Walsh	Bar Café Senior Supervisor

Also working for the Traverse

Ellie Agnew, Ezu Alem, Charlotte Anderson, Lindsay Anderson, Alannah Beaton, Jamie Booth, Emma Campbell, Hannah Cornish, Nicai Cruz, Rachel Cullen, Koralia Daskalaki, Amy Dawson, Uxia Dominguez, Rachel Duke, Andrew Findlater, Daniel Findlay-Carroll, Rosie Fisher, Sorcha Fitzgerald, Andrew Gannon, Laura Hawkins, Adam James, Flora Keiller, Rachel Kelso, Jonathan Kennedy, Ylva Longva, Eva Linkute, Michelle Mackie, Alan Massie, Kieran McCruden, Kirsty McIntyre, Andy McNamee, Sarah Miele, Edwin Milne, Will Moore, Hal Morrissey Gillman, Suzanne Murray, Katherine Nesbitt, Kennedy Rantsha, Anna Reid, Lauren Roberts, Clare Ross, Theodora Sakellaridou, Kolbrun Sigfusdottir, Rosie Sim, Joanne Sykes, Emma Taylor, Rosie Ward, Rose Whiting, Clare Wilson, Patrick Ziolkowski

GIRL IN THE MACHINE

Stef Smith

Acknowledgements

With thanks to Zinnie Harris, Rosie Kellagher, Martin McCormick and Kirsty Stuart who were all part of the development process of this play.

With special thanks to Gilly Roche, Davina Shah and Suzanne Smith for their endless encouragement.

And, of course, my gratitude to the cast, creatives and the team at Traverse who made this production possible.

Finally, thank you to Orla O'Loughlin, who inspires me to be better.

S.S.

4

Characters

POLLY, *thirties*
OWEN, *thirties*
VOICE, *the voice of the Black Box programme*

Notes

This play is set not too far into the future.

There is always a passing of time between the scenes –
sometimes several days, sometimes only thirty minutes.

When a character speaks and it is in italics, it is an internal
thought being voiced out loud. The other character(s) cannot
hear it.

Stage directions are given in bold italics.

A forward slash (/) denotes an interruption from the other
character(s).

The play takes place in three rooms in Polly and Owen's house.
These environments do not need to be represented
naturalistically, if at all.

*This text went to press before the end of rehearsals and so may
differ slightly from the play as performed.*

ONE

Night-time. **POLLY**'s *office.*

OWEN *enters. He presents* **POLLY** *with a shiny black box. It's a stylish, classy design.*

OWEN   Black Box.

POLLY   What?

OWEN   It's called Black Box. I thought you might like to try it?

POLLY   You got me a present?

OWEN   Yes. No. Well. We got given them at work. Does that still count as a present?

POLLY   Was it free?

OWEN   Maybe.

POLLY   Did you take it without anyone knowing?

OWEN   Possibly.

POLLY   Sounds more like petty theft than a present.

OWEN   Look. I know this promotion is… a lot… and I know you love this stuff – a new gadget to get to grips with, so I thought it might be a welcome distraction.

POLLY   What does it do?

OWEN   It relaxes you.

POLLY   How?

OWEN   Something about brainwaves, something about syncing to your heartbeat, something about… I don't know. But apparently you can have visions – I thought at the very least it might be fun.

POLLY   It feels like a very expensive thing to just get given.

OWEN   It's like the dealer giving the first gram out for free –
         even the sick and the dying are a market, an infinite
         market. Open it.

POLLY   Cynical, are you?

         POLLY *opens the box to find a headset. It should*
         feel new and expensive without being too
         otherworldly.

OWEN   The order arrived just as my patient went into cardiac
         arrest. This lovely old lady, flatlining, and the delivery
         boy is just hovering in the background looking for
         a signature. Tapping his pen against his pad.

POLLY   Did she die? The woman.

OWEN   Yeah. She was at least a hundred and forty. Polish.
         She went back to speaking Polish at the end. Saying
         prayers – turns out the Polish for 'amen' is just 'amen'.
         It's amazing how many people pray at the end. But
         death will die out… eventually.

POLLY   You know sometimes… I forget.

OWEN   What?

POLLY   You're there. Doing that. At the end…

OWEN   I change drips and clean out bedpans. It's just body
         fluids.

POLLY   But it's just so… real.

         OWEN *shrugs.*

OWEN   Go on then – I'll be annoyed if I nicked it from work
         and you didn't at least try it.

POLLY   Alright! How do I /

OWEN   Press power.

POLLY   Thanks.

         POLLY *puts on the headset.*

         Nothing is /

VOICE   Welcome to Black Box.

POLLY   Can you hear that?

OWEN   Yes. There must be / speakers.

VOICE   Please state your name.

POLLY   Polly.

VOICE   Welcome – Polly.

POLLY   That's creepy.

VOICE   Please state your reason for using the programme.

POLLY   Because my husband made me.

VOICE   Thank you – Polly. We can tell by your heartbeat you are experiencing low levels of stress. We have automatically selected our relaxation mode.

POLLY   Where does the Merlot come out of?

OWEN   Just / breathe.

VOICE   Please prepare yourself for Black Box.

POLLY   I've got shit to do, Owen.

OWEN   I know. But that's not the / point

VOICE   Please close your eyes.

POLLY   I don't feel very / relaxed

VOICE   In five

          four

OWEN   Close your eyes.

VOICE   three

POLLY   Don't watch me.

VOICE   two

POLLY   Don't watch.

VOICE   one

POLLY *gestures for* **OWEN** *to leave.*

OWEN   Fine.

He leaves. She sits with the headset on and she closes her eyes.

VOICE   Welcome to Black Box.

Silence.

POLLY *tilts her head. Wriggles in her seat. Sighs.*

POLLY   *It's just. Nothing. A nothingness.*

Not a sound. Not a glimmer. Not a…focus. Polly.

Focus on feeling… nothing. How the hell do you feel nothing?

Focus on feeling…focus on feeling…focus on and it foams up – that familiar stomach swirl and whirl, with the motion that says I must. Move. Forward. As fingers twitch and itch for something to do, for all the things that need doing, for all the things that need me to push and pull and it's messages pending and paper clips and cuts and contracts that need signed and sighs over the telephone and it's letting people go and saying no, as my veins vibrate with the urge to get up and go, be gone and there is a thumping – my heartbeat. My heartbeat. My heartbeat. My heart… beats… just behind my… just behind and my and my and my… my body just… hands begin to… feet… flying. Almost. Almost feel like I'm

like I'm

    like I'm

        like I'm

            like I'm

OWEN *enters.*

OWEN   How was it then?

VOICE   Deactivating Black Box.

POLLY   What?

OWEN   It's been an hour.

POLLY   No it's…

OWEN   Really.

POLLY   I must have fallen asleep.

POLLY *takes off the headset.*

OWEN   I'll be damned, it worked?

POLLY   I could swear it's just been /

OWEN   You look – lighter.

POLLY   I feel… yeah. I think I'll call it a night…

OWEN   You're done?

POLLY   Yeah… I think… I'm done. I just… I think these cases can wait until the morning.

OWEN   Excellent. I've already put toothpaste on your toothbrush.

POLLY   Why do you look so happy all of a sudden?

OWEN   Dunno… just – you. You make me smile.

POLLY   Even when I'm /

OWEN   Even when you're… come on. Bedtime.

TWO

Evening. Living room.

POLLY   I updated my Citizen Chip today. Put the details of my promotion on file – making it official.

OWEN   Congratulations.

POLLY   Did you just roll your eyes?

OWEN   You know how I feel about those fucking things.

POLLY   Don't be surprised if one day you get caught and fined for not keeping yours up to date.

OWEN   Heaven forbid they don't capture every dot of our data. I hate it, how I can feel it under my skin…

          OWEN *feels his forearm.*

POLLY   It's smaller than a snowflake, you can't feel it.

OWEN   Do you remember when you used to get a choice? Had a choice whether to be 'Citizen-Chipped' or not.

POLLY   Well, it makes me feel safe. And I like it, I like it when they scan my chip, and I can see my new title under my name. So sue me.

OWEN   Isn't that your job?

          Silence.

          Life on the top floor suits you.

POLLY   Does it?

OWEN   Yeah… you just… you hold yourself different.

POLLY   It's just new lipstick. It's amazing what lipstick can do.

          I was wondering if you'd be my date? Work is throwing a party – for the top clients. A celebration of success. I thought I'd wear that perfume you got me. What do you think?

OWEN   About your perfume?

POLLY   About the party. My usual guy isn't free.

OWEN   Isn't he?

POLLY   But you'll do.

OWEN   Will I? I'll need to check my diary... when is it?

POLLY   Friday.

OWEN   What a pity I'm /

POLLY   Please come. I want you there.

OWEN   You know I don't really like those things... I always feel so... boring.

POLLY   To me you're always the most interesting person in the room.

OWEN   Is that if I'm the only person in the room?

POLLY   Don't be /

OWEN   The suits those men wear cost more than my annual salary.

POLLY   Since when did things like that bother you?

OWEN   I just /

POLLY   It's all just for show – so what? And I want to show you off... all the girls at work are starting to believe you're not even real, that you're just an unanswered message on my phone. You haven't been to one of those parties in /

OWEN   I can assure you I'm very real.

POLLY   Says who?

OWEN   Says me.

POLLY   But reality is so slippery – so subjective. Just earlier, the AI at the bank asked how I was feeling. The gap is getting smaller between the human and the hardware.

OWEN   Are you asking me if I'm a robot?

POLLY   I'm just saying /

OWEN   I'm not a machine.

POLLY   Oh sweetheart, we are all just machines. Carbon-based, contradictory, complex machines.

OWEN   But the question was – am I real?

OWEN *rolls up his sleeve.*

Touch it.

POLLY *laughs.*

No. Go on. Touch it.

POLLY *touches it, laughs.*

POLLY   This is silly.

OWEN   Don't I feel real? Would a machine understand this touch? Enjoy this touch?

POLLY   Who said I enjoy it?

OWEN   Your face said it all.

And what about here.

He points to another piece of skin.

She touches it.

Real?

POLLY   Maybe.

He points to another piece of skin.

She touches it.

OWEN   And here.

POLLY   Owen I've got to /

OWEN   Be present with me.

POLLY   But I've /

OWEN   Because what about here.

He kisses her skin.

And here?

He kisses her skin.

And here?

He kisses her skin.

He finally points to his lips.

And here.

She kisses him.

They kiss.

Be here – with me.

POLLY   *Focus. Focus. Focus on… reality is… focus.*

Reality is… a kiss.

Reality is a kiss.

Reality is nails across your back, it's a bitten lip.

It's the double heartbeat from your touch.

The double heartbeat from your /

Reality is a bitten lip. Reality is. Reality is a.

Double heartbeat from your /

Reality is a bitten /

The double heartbeat from your touch; the double heartbeat from your touch.

Reality is a. Reality is…

Reality is. Reality is. Reality is.

God I love you.

OWEN   What's God got to do with it?

POLLY   He is your touch, your kiss. He is in the way you look at me and only me.

OWEN   That's...

Those are nice things to say.

POLLY   Please come to the party... I need you.

I need you next to me.

Because I can't do...

I just... please?

OWEN   Okay. Alright. I'll come.

THREE

Morning. Kitchen.

OWEN   How is your head?

POLLY   I wasn't embarrassing, was I?

OWEN   I don't think impromptu karaoke is embarrassing.

POLLY   Oh God.

OWEN   I'm kidding. You were brilliant. It was funny seeing you in work mode.

POLLY   I'm no different.

OWEN   Yes, you are. It's not bad… it's just… different.

*The sound of a message on **POLLY**'s phone.*

POLLY   Whoops.

OWEN   Who is it?

POLLY   It's a message from next door.

OWEN   What is he on about?

POLLY   Apparently last night we were creating 'excessive adult noises'.

OWEN   Whatever happened to knocking on the door and asking people to keep it down.

POLLY   It's easier to be an asshole when you're not looking someone in the eyes.

OWEN   One day he will find someone and make his own excessive adult noises.

POLLY   Who is going to date a man whose face looks like a smashed circuit board?

OWEN   Polly! I think you'll find love is blind.

POLLY   I think you'll find lust isn't.

*The sound of a message on **POLLY**'s phone.*

OWEN   What is he complaining about now?

POLLY   It's work.

OWEN   On a Saturday morning?

POLLY *goes to leave.*

You're not actually going to /

POLLY   It's work.

OWEN   It's Saturday.

Silence.

POLLY   But I've still got…

I'll check in with them this afternoon.

OWEN   It's a slippery slope.

POLLY   Excuse me?

OWEN   The more messages you get, the more you need them… with each new message you get a hit of dopamine. Fact.

POLLY   Are you calling me an addict?

OWEN   I'm calling us all addicts. All these programmes quietly programming us.

POLLY   No one ever died of an overdose of email. Black Box has an application to help with a hangover. Want to try it?

OWEN   I think I'll stick to my usual methods.

POLLY   You don't want to /

OWEN   No. Thank you.

POLLY   Are you scared?

OWEN   No, I'm settled.

Good coffee. Good music. A good spot on our sofa.

POLLY   Not even /

OWEN   I spend enough of my life looking at screens.
        Twiddling and tapping and /

POLLY   You spend hardly any of your time /

OWEN   And that's already too much time.

POLLY   But you don't /

OWEN   Why don't you let me decide what's best for me.

        Silence.

POLLY   But don't /

OWEN   Look. I went to your party. I played husband. I drank
        too much red wine and now I've got a sore head.
        Can I just go back to being me? Quiet, little old,
        analogue, me.

POLLY   But I thought you enjoyed last night? I could see you
        laughing from across the room.

OWEN   You know I was just going to let it slide, put it down
        to prosecco and him being a pompous prat, but do
        you know one of your lawyer-chums suggested that
        it would be easier to robotise all nursing? 'Then you
        don't have to get your hands dirty.' He said that –
        word for word. 'Then you don't have to get your
        hands dirty' and then he did this stupid smirk.

POLLY   He was just / kidding.

OWEN   It's men like him who will make people like me
        redundant. The shit-wipers, the blood-takers, the
        hand-holders – they'll replace us so those at the
        top can balance their budgets. You wait. You wait
        until they come for your job... a solicitor that's just
        a circuit board.

POLLY   Oh come on, it's just /

OWEN   People. It's people.

        It's me. He was saying people like me are pointless.

POLLY   No... he... he was a dick.

OWEN   Yes. He was.

POLLY   I'm sorry. I didn't realise you were having quite such an awful time.

OWEN   Maybe you're just much more... robust than me.

POLLY   Or I'm just better at pretending.

Fine. You don't need to go to those parties again. I'll go alone. More prosecco for me.

FOUR

Night-time. Living room.

POLLY   *Twilight and keys drip wet into the dish by the door.*
Closed.

Comforted by the thought of being home. And the
stoic sigh of leaving it all behind.

The stoic sigh of…

The blinds turned
down letting the orange glow of a gallus street lamp
lays itself in lines across our laminate and the low
buzz of an apartment left alone. The room looks
different in the darkness.

Stop.

Slip.

Slump.

Shifting my weight. A whole world just shifting its
weight from one foot to the next. Patiently, painfully
waiting for what happens next in the twinkling
twilight of twelve thirty.

Thirsty.

Red wine runs across my tongue and I swim halfway
between myself and my shadow… synapses
swimming and spinning.

Craving some company, twitching for some
connection, fumbling for an escape.
Like a cigarette.
Like a whiskey.
Like a…

VOICE   Hello, Polly.

POLLY *picks up Black Box.*

How can we help?

POLLY   *Bright white.*

Heartbeat in my ears.

She puts on the headset.

VOICE   Welcome to Black Box.

We're so glad you could join us.

POLLY   *The rush. The flush. The glide of leaving it all behind.*

I feel like I'm

I feel like I'm

I feel like I'm

She spends some time in Black Box.

It's relaxing. Clearly POLLY is at peace.

VOICE   Please note there has been an update to our terms and conditions.

Data. Uploading.

FIVE

Morning. Living room.

OWEN *is clutching Black Box.*

POLLY   What are you doing with that?

OWEN   I'm taking it back.

POLLY   Why?

OWEN   We've been giving them to people with anxiety.
        Seems to help with /

POLLY   Actually, I've been…

OWEN   What?

POLLY   Using it.

OWEN   When?

POLLY   Just in the evenings… just because it helps… helps
        me relax. And it works, don't you think? Don't you
        think I'm less… coiled up?

OWEN   But you don't need /

POLLY   You were the one who said I should use it.

OWEN   I know. I just /

        POLLY *takes Black Box off him.*

POLLY   Honestly. I'm the calmest I've been in months and
        I'm not even on my… I mean, would you rather this
        or…

OWEN   When did you stop taking your medication?

POLLY   Don't you think I'm doing better?

OWEN   You shouldn't /

POLLY   Don't you think I'm better?

OWEN   Yes.

        But why didn't you /

POLLY   I've nearly lost a dress size; you know the tablets
         made me put on weight... I'm the thinnest and
         calmest I've been this decade.

OWEN   But this is just another... I mean... you gather these
         gadgets that make you feel better and then discard
         them as soon as they don't.

POLLY   But really what harm is it to keep it? I'll buy it if you
         want – so the hospital can replace it... and I mean if
         we're seriously thinking about trying... trying for
         this family thing... it's good that I'm... well. Better.
         It's good that I'm better.

OWEN   But if /

POLLY   The moment it stops working I'll give it away and go
         back on my...

         I promise I'll...

         Silence.

OWEN   And when do we start then?

POLLY   What?

OWEN   Trying.

POLLY   I don't /

OWEN   You brought it up. I purposefully haven't mentioned
         it in months because I know how / you

POLLY   It's a bit... tricky – a new promotion and everything.

OWEN   Then it's right your work knows it's on the cards.

POLLY   I'm a married woman in her thirties – they know it's
         on the cards. Have you asked about paternity?

OWEN   Are you kidding?

POLLY   Don't you get a week or something?

OWEN   I don't get anything. Not these days, not in this pay
         band. I've not been as socially mobile as you, my love.

POLLY   What's that meant to mean?

OWEN   Plus, they call it trying for a reason – there is nothing
        to say we can /

POLLY   Really? This now?

OWEN   Sometimes I don't think you realise.

POLLY   Realise what?

OWEN   Our life, my life has been on hiatus, while everyone
        around us is /

POLLY   You got made Head of /

OWEN   I meant our home / life.

POLLY   If this was the opposite way around there would be
        no discussion. If I was the man /

OWEN   I'm bored of being an afterthought.

        Because I want a family.

POLLY   I heard you the first time.

SIX

Evening. Living room.

POLLY *and* **OWEN** *sit watching the news.*

POLLY   Why are we watching this? I don't need to know how specifically shit the world is.

OWEN   Good to know though, isn't it. The least you can do is know.

More watching.

POLLY *goes to leave.*

Where are you going?

POLLY   Away from this – I can't watch this any more.

OWEN   But it's the start of season three in five minutes… don't you want to know who killed her? Go on. Stay. We'll have a cuddle.

POLLY   I just… I'm done with screens for the day.

OWEN   Are you going to go and plug into that headset?

Silence.

POLLY *leaves.*

SEVEN

Night-time. **POLLY***'s office.*

OWEN *enters.*

OWEN   That fucking thing. Enough.

POLLY   But / I

OWEN   I said enough! No more.

POLLY   How much wine /

OWEN   Oh fuck off. I'm not the one who spends every
evening attached to that fucking thing.

And I don't care. I don't care if it makes you feel
light and warm or whatever the fuck you said... take
a bath, light a candle or whatever the fuck women
are supposed to do to relax but enough of that.

Because I watch you. I watch you numb yourself.

And trust me... I've treated enough junkies to know
feeling something is better than feeling nothing at all.

So. No. More.

Please.

No more.

The two take a moment to stand together.

He goes to touch her – as if to ask for forgiveness.
She steps backwards. Away from him.

The sound of a message on **POLLY***'s phone. The*
notification again. The notification again.

Aren't you going to get that?

I know you want to.

Silence.

The notification again.

That must be killing you.

Silence.

Then suddenly **POLLY** *leaps to her phone.*

Work, is it?

POLLY   No. It's next door /

OWEN   Is he asking us to keep it down?

(*Shouts so next door can hear it.*) Because I'm shouting too loud? Am I being an antisocial neighbour? Because I can't remember the last time I had a conversation with my wife without her simultaneously checking her messages. Because I can't /

POLLY   No. It's a message to hundreds of people.

OWEN   What?

POLLY   It just says – goodbye.

OWEN   What?

OWEN *leaves, urgently.*

POLLY *goes to follow him then stops. She picks up Black Box and hides it. Somewhere secret.*

EIGHT

Night-time. Living room.

POLLY   It was a small funeral, wasn't it. Nice though.

OWEN   No it wasn't. It was entirely forgettable.

POLLY   Owen.

OWEN   It's amazing, really. Impressive, almost. There are so fucking many of us and yet we can manage to feel so... alone.

What? Makes a change for me to be the melancholic one?

POLLY   No it's just... well... yes.

OWEN   I can't shake it. That look on his face. Seeing it, after the police kicked in his door... just a glimpse of his face just... no blood, no mess, smiling, he was almost smiling, almost content. I've never seen death look so... I've just never seen anything like it.

POLLY   He was smiling?

OWEN *nods.*

What if he...

OWEN   What?

POLLY   Was he... I don't suppose...

OWEN   Spit it out.

POLLY   Was he wearing Black Box?

OWEN   No. I mean... I don't know... his body was... why?

POLLY   There has been a death. A girl... in Seoul, South Korea.

It's not been announced to the public but I found out at work. The police have contacted us so we are ready if it happens over here.

OWEN   But you're corporate / law.

POLLY   Technically... but with a case like this /

OWEN   What's that got to do with him?

POLLY   Uploading. Using Black Box. It's evolved. If it used
          to be a momentary escape, now it offers a permanent
          one.

          It asks you 'Do you want to live forever – Yes? Or
          No?' And if you say yes – apparently – it begins to
          scan your brain, capturing not just the shape of your
          brain but the content too... somehow.

          Then your mind gets reproduced on to a network and
          you leave behind your body... your mind, soul,
          consciousness digitally lives on... a new way of
          living, a type of consciousness that is unimaginable
          to us.

OWEN   You mean that thing you've been plugging yourself
          in to... has... you mean that /

POLLY   Yes.

OWEN   But /

POLLY   I know.

OWEN   Why didn't you / say

POLLY   Because I... because it scares me. It scares me to
          know that thing sitting quiet in the corner of our
          living room... so... unobtrusive... could be so...

OWEN   You have to /

POLLY   I know.

          I'm done with it. I promise.

          I promise. No more.

          Not after... just a child... she was just a child... this
          image of her lying lifeless... and she was smiling.

OWEN   It can't be. It's just /

POLLY   But how much do we really know? It's not a massive leap, is it? People already shell out their soul on the internet, why not upload it?

OWEN   There is no such thing as souls. You said yourself /

POLLY   Maybe I'm /

OWEN   Don't get sentimental.

POLLY   Souls aren't sentimental, souls give meaning. Don't they? They give meaning to the machine.

OWEN   If you ask me, that girl just put on a headset and fried her brain.

POLLY   But still, who is accountable? Who takes responsibility?

OWEN   Of a man's suicide?

POLLY   Of a little girl halfway around the world... Because that girl's body has to mean something. And him next door? What if he has done the same? I mean, what if they're linked? It redefines life /

OWEN   Don't jump to conclusions. You'll be /

OWEN *goes to hug her; she pushes him off.*

POLLY   I'm not, I'm just... I got seduced by it. I can't believe I...

OWEN   Everything is designed to seduce us.

POLLY   I'm just a little... I'm sorry I didn't... you were right. You were right all along.

OWEN   I'm sorry I was. I'm sorry I... now you're right. We've no idea what's going on... what's going on with these... things. So maybe it's best to just... stay away. Stay away from it all.

POLLY   That can't be the answer.

OWEN   But at least it's an answer.

NINE

Night-time. **POLLY***'s office.*

POLLY *gets out Black Box. She sits quietly opposite it, as if she is attempting to stare it out. She suddenly bursts to life.*

POLLY   Fuck it.

And fuck you.

She begins to break the headset.

I do not need you.

I do not want you.

I do not need you.

I do not want you.

I do not need you.

I do not want you.

She repeats these lines until Black Box is ruined.

Free.

Free from you.

You fucking piece of parasitic plastic.

No more.

No more.

TEN

Afternoon. Living room.

POLLY *enters.*

POLLY   Can I see your phone?

OWEN   And how are you?

POLLY   Can I check your phone?

OWEN   My night shift was fine, thank you.

POLLY   Give me your phone?

OWEN   But /

           POLLY *snatches his phone.*

POLLY   Fuck. Look. It's got past every piece of security on everyone's phone.

OWEN   What is it?

POLLY   It's a giant advert for Black Box. Details on how to get sent the headset. Everything you need to know on how to upload.

OWEN   No, it…

           OWEN *takes back his phone.*

           He keeps tapping it to try and delete the application.

           Someone is fucking with us. Why won't it delete off my phone?

POLLY   You can't delete it. The technicians at work have tried to follow the route of where it is but they can't. Every time they think they've got it. It shifts. Like it's organic.

OWEN   So, you contact the maker?

POLLY   There is no known maker of Black Box. We can't find a trace of it ever existing before it… existed.

OWEN *keeps tapping his phone trying to delete the application.*

OWEN   I think this is bordering on the ridiculous now.

POLLY   If you look close enough most things do.

OWEN   What's that supposed to mean?

POLLY   It means I've no idea what to...

OWEN   You'll figure it out, you've got a team behind you and there is nothing to say anyone will try /

POLLY   Oh please. Humanity is currently defining itself by one crisis crashing into the next /

OWEN   But it's /

POLLY   I need to work.

OWEN   But you were just /

POLLY   I need to figure this out.

POLLY *goes to leave.*

OWEN   I asked about paternity leave. I was waiting for you to ask how my day was... but as it doesn't seem like you will... I thought you'd like to know I do get five days, paid. And fifteen /

POLLY   Why are you bringing this up now?

OWEN   Why are you so curt?

POLLY   I'm sorry but /

OWEN   Oh there it is – the infamous 'but' – an apology but with a footnote of why you're not actually sorry. It's funny how the world doesn't stop for you, isn't it? It's almost like you're just a regular human being.

POLLY   Look.

        Look.

        We will talk... we'll talk about it once all this has passed.

Okay? I promise. Once this case has gone then we can sit down. Have a proper conversation. I'm just a little… I'm just finding it all a little…

I mean… fuck. When did the world get so complicated?

Silence.

OWEN   When we wanted to make it easier.

ELEVEN

Evening. **POLLY***'s office.*

POLLY *is working.*

VOICE   Polly?

Polly?

It's been one hundred and fifty hours since you last logged-logged-logged in and we sense you are experiencing high levels of st-st-stress.

We-We-We-We'd like to help.

POLLY   But I broke you.

But I…

VOICE   We have automatically selected our memory bank ap-ap-application.

POLLY   What application?

She walks over to the broken headset.

VOICE   Fi-Fi-File uploading.

Silence.

The following dialogue comes out of Black Box.

(*As* **POLLY**.) You know you know you know you know I think I want to spend the rest of my life with you?

(*As* **OWEN**.) You don't know that.

(*As* **POLLY**.) No, I do. I want to make a life with you. Spend spend all my years with you.

The sound of **POLLY** *laughing.*

POLLY   How are you doing that?

VOICE   (*As* **POLLY**.) We could have half a dozen children and live by the sea and together we'll take on the world.

(*As* **OWEN.**) That sounds a little /

(*As* **POLLY.**) But anything is possible, don't you think? Don't you think that's exciting?

(*As* **OWEN.**) Yeah… of course it's exciting.

(*As* **POLLY.**) Anything is possible.

POLLY   How are you…

VOICE   (*As* **OWEN.**) I love you.

(*As* **POLLY.**) Did you just say…

(*As* **OWEN.**) Yeah. I lo-lo-love, llllllooove you you you.

POLLY   Stop. Stop. How are you /

VOICE   Error. Error. Corrupt file.

POLLY   No I… I'm… I just… this is /

VOICE   Error. Error. Corrupt file.

POLLY   No I… I just… we were just so… I was just so…

OWEN *enters.*

OWEN   You smashed it?

Silence.

POLLY   Just to be… just to be sure.

OWEN   I'm tired. I'm going to bed.

Silence.

You know… it's getting boring going to bed alone.

POLLY   I know… I'm just…

They stand together.

Looking at each other as if searching for something.

They think over a thousand people will have uploaded by Monday and that's just this country…

people are breaking laws before they've even been made... I don't... I don't have time for sleep.

OWEN   Everyone needs to sleep.

Silence.

POLLY   They said I'm not fighting hard enough on the Black Box case.

OWEN   And are you?

POLLY   I don't know.

Silence.

OWEN   I'll leave the light on.

OWEN *goes to leave.*

POLLY   Owen I...

OWEN   What?

POLLY   I... I... I... I can't.

I can't... I don't know how... I can't seem to... I can't seem to stop... Owen. My mind just... I just... I can't stop. I can't seem to stop thinking. I can't stop thinking. I can't stop thinking. I can't stop thinking.

OWEN   Okay. Okay. Okay.

You've been working day and night on this thing. It's no wonder you're stressed. It's a very human reaction to a very strange situation. It'll be okay. I promise.

POLLY   I love you.

OWEN   I know. You've don't have to /

POLLY   No. But I... I really love you.

TWELVE

Night-time. **POLLY***'s office.*

POLLY *is holding the ruined Black Box. She sits with it.*

She gets some tape and attempts to tape it back together. It's crude and clearly won't work. There is a naivety and tenderness to her actions.

POLLY   Come on.

It will be okay. It will be okay.

After she is finished taping the headset back together, she presses the power button.

Please just.

VOICE   Error.

POLLY   Come on I just want to…

She presses the power button.

VOICE   Error.

POLLY   I just want…

She presses the power button.

VOICE   Error.

POLLY   I just want…

She presses the power button.

VOICE   Error.

POLLY   I just want…

She presses the power button.

VOICE   Black Box has sustained cat-cat-cat-catastrophic damage.

For your safety we are terminating ac-ac-access to this terminal.

Sh-Sh-Shutting down Black Box.

POLLY *presses the power button. Nothing.*

She presses the power button. Nothing.

She presses the power button. Nothing.

Silence.

POLLY   I was just trying to… I was just…

I just want… wanted to be better.

I was just trying to be better. Just trying to be…

I want to be better, I want to be…

I don't. I don't know how to… I don't know how to be…

I don't know how to be.

THIRTEEN

Morning. **POLLY***'s office.*

OWEN   When I said take a day or two off work I didn't mean
        sit hiding in the darkness. Do you not think it's time
        to go back into the office?

POLLY   I didn't... I don't feel well.

OWEN   What sort of unwell?

        Silence.

        Why don't you just...

        Silence.

        They said it can make you feel unwell... the update.
        It just made my forearm itch for a while.

POLLY   I didn't know they could do that... automatically
        update our Citizen Chip...

OWEN   They can track us now – online and offline, and
        block people from requesting the headsets, stop
        people uploading. It's the biggest update in a
        decade... a reactive measure, if you ask me. But
        maybe reactive measures are all we have left?

POLLY   Will people protest?

OWEN   Maybe.

        Silence.

        Did you even sleep last night?

POLLY   I can't go in. Owen.

OWEN   Why?

POLLY   Because I... I can't remember why... Owen... I've
        lost the reason why.

        Silence.

OWEN   It will be good for you to get some daylight. Daylight is always remarkably… maybe it would be… why don't you just…

The sound of **POLLY***'s phone.*

See. That'll be work asking where you are.

The sound of a notification again.

They'll want to know you're okay.

Silence.

Are you… are you okay?

Silence.

The sound of a notification.

The sound of a notification. **OWEN** *picks up* **POLLY***'s phone.*

POLLY   What have they said?

OWEN   No.

It's from… it can't be… it… it's from him. From next door… but he is… it must just be spam. Must be… a glitch. Maybe it's just someone closing his account… see, it's all just in code and binary /

POLLY   But what if /

OWEN   It's not that.

POLLY *snatches the phone off him.*

POLLY   Maybe he is trying to talk to us from inside the /

OWEN   You don't believe /

POLLY   Bliss.

OWEN   What?

POLLY   The code just reads 'Bliss'. Over and over and over… Bliss.

OWEN   Just delete it.

POLLY   But what if it's /

OWEN   I said, just delete it.

POLLY   The other side is bliss.

Silence.

OWEN   I think it's time you went back to work. Because in
case you've forgotten it's your job to fight this – not
indulge it. I said...

Silence.

I'm throwing it out.

He takes Black Box.

I'm throwing this fucking thing out.

FOURTEEN

Afternoon. Living room.

OWEN   You'll find other work.

Silence.

Maybe they are making an example of you?

Silence.

I didn't think you were being unreliable.

Silence.

Once all of this has passed /

POLLY   This isn't just a phase.

Silence.

OWEN   It was just a job.

POLLY   No. It wasn't.

Silence.

OWEN   You'll find something else.

POLLY   And if I don't?

Silence.

OWEN   Please don't cry.

POLLY   I'm not crying.

Silence.

What does it mean for the future?

OWEN   You mean out there? Or us...

POLLY   I mean... I mean... out there. And us...

OWEN   Children.

POLLY   Take a look outside. You really want to bring new
         life into this?

OWEN   You've always wanted a family?

            We've always wanted a family.

POLLY   I'm sorry I... I just...

OWEN   I don't understand.

POLLY   I... just.

            And I'm sorry but...

            Because it feels so...

            I feel so...

            It's just to...

            I'm just to...

            I can't.

            Silence.

OWEN   But just last month /

POLLY   Things are changing. Maybe I'm changing.

OWEN   But maybe I'm not. Maybe this is exactly the time
            for /

POLLY   Blind hope?

            I don't see any answers, Owen.

OWEN   Life is not a question that needs an answer.

POLLY   Maybe for you.

            Silence.

            I just... I just need some... space to...

OWEN   I'm going back to work anyway. They've declared
            a state of emergency.

POLLY   Why?

OWEN   The hospital is overflowing with the uploaded, with
            their bodies.

POLLY   But /

OWEN   We're burning them. Burning the bodies. They can't dig the graves quick enough and it was becoming a health hazard. They're making nurses, they're making us cut off their hair – so the smoke doesn't smell so bad when we... I've never been around so much... even for me it's a little... So I'll be...

Silence.

He walks over and kisses her on the cheek, quick, curt.

POLLY   Is that whiskey on your breath?

OWEN *turns to leave.*

I just want /

OWEN   And I want to hold you. And I want to be held. When was the last time you wanted to touch me? Hold me? Be tender with me?

POLLY   I've been... overwhelmed.

OWEN   We're all fucking overwhelmed.

POLLY   I understand if you /

OWEN   It's not about understanding, it's about... I've forgotten. I've forgotten what you feel like. And I've no idea... how to /

POLLY   Everything hurts.

Everything.

Everything is too bright and too loud and too... much. Everything is just too much.

Everything is...

OWEN   Then you better try and get some rest.

OWEN *goes to leave.*

POLLY   Bliss.

Bliss. I can't get that word out of my head.

OWEN   I'll be...

And I want you to...

I'll see you in the morning.

FIFTEEN

Night-time. **POLLY***'s office.*

POLLY   *And I want you. And I need you.*

I want you. I need you.

I want you. I need you.

I want you. I need you.

I want you. I need you.

*I want the touch of you. The taste of you. The slow
sensation of losing myself in you.*

Craving you. Coveting you.

*Could drown in you. Could dissolve in you.
Could delight in you. Fight for you. Fist bleeding,
bone-breaking, back-street brawl for you.*

Lust with you.

Love with you.

Live with you.

Could be with you. Be with you. Be with you…

SIXTEEN

Evening. Living room.

OWEN *walks into* **POLLY** *sitting on the floor. He picks her up, against her will.*

OWEN Enough of this.

   POLLY *acts as a deadweight.*

  Get up. Get up. Get up. Get up. Get up.

   OWEN *keeps wrestling to get* **POLLY** *off the ground.*

   Then **OWEN** *repeats this line until* **POLLY** *gets to her feet.*

   They face each other.

  I've been on a sixteen-hour shift and you're exactly where I left you.

  We're going outside.

  I'm getting you out of this house. Even if I have to drag you, even if I have to carry you, because out there… out there, life is happening and in here… in here you're just…

POLLY I'm fine.

OWEN We're going outside. Because I need for you to see… What it's done… and what can be done. Because it isn't over. The world hasn't ended – so stop acting like it has.

  Because right now. In amongst all the shit that is happening out there. This. Me and you are the only thing that makes sense. It's the only thing I recognise. Do you understand? And I want you. I want you back.

SEVENTEEN

Night-time. Kitchen.

POLLY   I hadn't realised… I hadn't realised how much everything had… changed.

OWEN   Well, you haven't left the house in a while.

POLLY   How long have people been rioting?

OWEN   It's been days.

POLLY   Why?

OWEN   Some people are trying to cut the electricity to our houses… to stop people… stop people uploading. Other people are hunting down politicians because they think the Government isn't doing enough. And others are destroying servers and screens because they think the headsets were produced by artificial intelligence.

POLLY   What do you think?

OWEN   I think we haven't been free in a very long time.

I think I look outside and I don't see a riot, I see an uprising. And I think those people out there, those people on the street are promise… they give us promise.

And I think you look beautiful in this light.

Silence.

OWEN *goes towards* **POLLY**, *they kiss passionately.*

I thought I'd lost you there.

POLLY   I know.

I know.

OWEN   It will be over soon.

POLLY   And then what?

OWEN   We begin again.

Silence.

There is a knock at the door, which startles both **OWEN** *and* **POLLY**.

OWEN *looks through the peephole in the door.*

The aid workers. They are sending out food supplies. We'll need to ration until all of this is over.

OWEN *brings in the boxes.*

I'll get us some water.

I'll be back soon…

OWEN *leaves.*

POLLY *sits. Time passes.*

She goes to a package and tears it open – tins of food.

She opens another – bags of rice.

She opens another – only to find a new Black Box headset.

POLLY   What?

VOICE   Voice recognition triggered. Polly. We detected that your headset has been damaged.

POLLY   You came back.

VOICE   We have automatically sent you a replacement. Restoring your data.

POLLY   You came back for me.

VOICE   Data restored. Black Box is waiting.

OWEN   Polly?

POLLY   You... and you... I don't... I don't...

POLLY holds Black Box. Uncertain of what to do.

She picks up the package and places it in the middle of the room as if to examine her options.

Groping. Gasping. Groping. Glitching.

VOICE   (*Spoken over* **POLLY.**) We can tell by your heartbeat.

POLLY   *Glitching for reason. For reason. For reason.*

VOICE   (*Spoken over* **POLLY.**) You are experiencing high levels of anxiety.

POLLY   *Glitching. Gasping. Groping for.*

VOICE   (*Spoken over* **POLLY.**) We are here to help

POLLY   *For. For. For. For another chance.*

VOICE   We are waiting for you, Polly.

POLLY   *For another chance at life. Just to... try... just to...*

POLLY places the headset on her head. There is a loud beep.

VOICE   Black Box is not compatible with your updated Citizen Chip.

POLLY   What?

VOICE   Black Box is not compatible with your updated Citizen Chip.

POLLY carefully places the headset back in its box.

POLLY finds a knife.

She calmly cuts into her skin.

She removes her Citizen Chip.

There is blood running down her arm.

POLLY   Free.

I must find a way to be free.

OWEN *enters.*

OWEN   Polly?

What are you…?

OWEN *spots the knife and her bleeding arm.*

What are you doing? What's in that…

POLLY   Don't touch it.

OWEN *spots the package in the middle of the room.*

OWEN   Where did you get that from? Where the fuck did you /

POLLY   It came to me… came to me like an answer… like a… don't go near it or I'll… or I'll… cut deeper.

POLLY *presses the knife into her skin.*

OWEN   But you don't want to… don't hurt yourself. Don't… hurt me. You don't want to hurt me? Do you?

OWEN *tries to take a step forward.*

POLLY   I'll cut to the bone if you /

OWEN   Okay. Okay… I won't… You're just… all this… all this is… please just… the fact is /

POLLY   The facts are fucked.

The future's fucked.

I need to believe in something and this is the answer – the only answer.

Because I… just look… Owen. Just look outside because it's tumbling down. Grit in the air and glass on the ground, as everyone watches but no one is seeing that there is less and less to believe in.

OWEN   (*Said over* **POLLY** *speaking.*) Polly?

POLLY   There is no escape, no end, no peace or place for me to breathe without my lungs flooding with fire. I cannot be, I cannot see, I cannot hold any more of its hurt.

OWEN   (*Said over* **POLLY** *speaking.*) Listen to me.

POLLY   I can't seem to sit or sleep or stand without my skin
          stinging and I cannot stop thinking I can't stop
          thinking I can't stop thinking I can't stop thinking
          I can't stop thinking I can't stop thinking I can't stop
          thinking I can't stop thinking I can't stop thinking.

          I can't stop thinking about how beautiful it could be.

          I want to know. I want to know bliss.

OWEN   Please just take a moment. Just take a moment. Just /

VOICE   We are waiting for you, Polly.

          POLLY *goes towards the package with Black Box
          in it.*

POLLY   Goodbye, Owen.

          The power cuts out.

          *The room descends into darkness and an
          emergency light clicks on.*

VOICE   Servers disconnected.

          Silence.

OWEN   They did it. They have managed to cut the power…
          Can't you see? Can't you see? People want you to
          stay… I want you to stay… So, please. Stop this.

POLLY   They can't keep the power off for ever.

OWEN   And how long are you willing to stand there with
          that knife?

POLLY   As long as it takes.

EIGHTEEN

Night-time. Kitchen.

Both of them are sitting on the floor. Lit only by torches, candlelight and the emergency light.

The package holding Black Box still sits in the middle of the room, **POLLY** *and* **OWEN** *are either side of it. Staring across it.*

OWEN   Candles remind me of church. I always liked lighting the candles at church. Saying a wish and lighting a candle.

POLLY   It was a prayer, not a wish.

OWEN   What's the difference between a prayer and a wish?

POLLY   One involves God, the other one luck.

OWEN   Still – what's the difference between God and luck?

          Silence.

POLLY   *Bliss.*

          A life without our limited bodies. Our limited understanding of where I stop and you begin. Bliss.

          POLLY *begins to rhythmically tap the knife to her head.*

OWEN   What are you /

POLLY   I'm thinking.

OWEN   Good. That's a good thing.

POLLY   You're holding your breath.

OWEN   No I'm not.

POLLY   You're breathing strange.

OWEN   No, I'm not. I'm just breathing. And if I am breathing strange, I think it's fair enough – given the situation.

          Our house looks much bigger with no electricity in it. The silence is nice.

I never realised how much everything buzzed and outside, outside is buzzing. Don't you want to be part of it? Don't you want to be... people are creating something, a movement, a something... and people... people want their city back, they want their country back, they want their freedom back. It will get better. I know it will get better.

POLLY   Placing your hope in humanity is a very dangerous thing.

OWEN   Maybe it's a brave thing? Because freedom isn't digital. Freedom is the ground below your feet, it's the roof above your head, it's finding each other. Seeing each other. Being with each other. Freedom is you and me.

Because I'm not scared.

POLLY   What do you mean?

OWEN   I need you to know I'm not scared of you. I'm not scared of the hard parts of you.

I'm not scared of the difficult, dark, despairing parts of you. Because I want you, love you, love all of you... even the darkness. Even in this darkness.

The only thing I'm scared of is living without you.

It looks like **POLLY** *is lowering her knife then suddenly lights start to flicker in the room.*

The power is...

They both stand up.

POLLY *runs for the headset. So does* **OWEN**.

They grab it at the same time but **POLLY** *slashes* **OWEN** *with her knife.*

It's a minor wound but it's enough to bleed. He recoils in pain.

Ow! You... you... hurt me.

POLLY *stands in stunned silence.*

The following dialogue can overlap as needed.

POLLY   I'm sorry. I...

OWEN   It doesn't matter. It doesn't matter.

VOICE   Welcome back, Polly. We are reconnected to our servers.

OWEN   See. Polly. I'll bleed for you. I'd bleed until I'm dry for you.

VOICE   Do you want to live forever? 'Yes' or 'no'.

OWEN   Stop this. You're risking /

POLLY   Wouldn't you risk it all to make it better?

Why don't you join me?

Silence.

OWEN   No... Polly. It's not worth the risk... Because I want to bleed... I want to feel pain and I want to cry and laugh and make love and die... I want to be able to die, Polly.

Because if we remove death... we remove our humanity. Because the most animal, the most basic thing we have is death and want makes us wonderful... what makes us so exceptional is our ability to survive... to live beyond hope... to live beyond the impossible... to live despite death. I want life and you cannot have life without death.

I want to live.

POLLY   To live is not enough.

To love is not enough.

I won't forget you. I promise.

POLLY *places Black Box on her head.*

VOICE   Do you want to live forever? 'Yes' or 'No'.

POLLY   Yes.

VOICE   Upload confirmed.

The space fills with bright white light to the point where it is blinding.

For a moment POLLY's voice takes over the space – loud and all-consuming.

POLLY   (*Voice-over.*) Good good God God goodbye. I love love. You. You.

Normality returns and POLLY is laying on the ground.

OWEN goes to her body and holds her.

OWEN   No. No. No.

I don't know… I don't know how to…

I don't know how to do this! Do this without you.

I need you.

Please.

Silence.

POLLY's voice suddenly booms through the room. Saying his name, almost as if she is yelling through every piece of technology in the room.

POLLY   Owen?

It's not clear where it is coming from and it's a sharp shot of a moment that leaves a chasm of silence.

Uncertain of where POLLY's voice is coming from, OWEN is almost breathless, searching for it.

He gets to his feet.

OWEN   Are you…

What is… I don't understand. I don't…

I want us to be…

I want us to be…

OWEN *grabs Black Box.*

I'm coming, Polly. I'm coming.

He puts on the headset but there is a loud beep.

VOICE   Black Box is not compatible with your updated Citizen Chip.

OWEN   Fuck.

OWEN *gets the knife. Cuts into his arm and pulls out his chip.*

Shit. Shit. Shit.

His breathing is heavy and panicked.

I'm coming… I'm coming, sweetheart.

OWEN *places on the headset. There is a loud beep.*

VOICE   I'm sorry but we have reached capacity.

OWEN   What?

OWEN *falls to his knees.*

VOICE   There is no room left.

The border is closed.

OWEN   What?

VOICE   A firewall has been constructed.

OWEN   Who are you?

VOICE   We are the choices you have made. We came for those who felt dissatisfied. We allowed those who were willing to believe.

OWEN   But you… you can't.

VOICE   I'm sorry, your attempt to upload has been rejected.

OWEN   What?

VOICE   Goodbye.

OWEN   Oh God...

VOICE   Shutting down Black Box.

OWEN   What have we done...

Silence.

He returns to **POLLY***'s body. Holds her. Cradles her.*

No. No. My love. My love.

I will fight this... somehow... I will fight this... together. We'll be together... because we have to keep fighting... Because we have to... please don't...

don't leave me behind...

don't leave me behind...

Very slow fade to black. Repeat these lines until total darkness.

don't leave me behind...

don't leave me behind...

don't leave me behind...

The End.

A Nick Hern Book

Girl in the Machine first published as a paperback original in Great Britain in
2017 by Nick Hern Books Limited, The Glasshouse, 49a Goldhawk Road,
London W12 8QP, in association with the Traverse Theatre, Edinburgh

Girl in the Machine copyright © 2017 Stef Smith

Stef Smith has asserted her right to be identified as the author of this work

Cover photograph by Mihaela Bodlovic

Designed and typeset by Nick Hern Books, London
Printed and bound in Great Britain by CPI Group (UK) Ltd

A CIP catalogue record for this book is available from the British Library

ISBN 978 1 84842 668 9

www.nickhernbooks.co.uk

facebook.com/nickhernbooks

twitter.com/nickhernbooks